How To Create Wealth

Destiny S. Harris

Support this work by leaving a review.

Enjoy A Free Gift At The End Of This Book

1st Free Gift!

Giving Rocks.

I give away free books daily. Get your free books today. Here's how

Step 1: Visit <u>amazon.com/author/destinyharris</u>

Step 2: Filter books by "Price: Low to High"

Step 3: Download available free books

Table of Contents

. . .

. . .

Chapter 1

Create A Wealth Mindset

Wealth starts from a seed within your mind.

How you think determines what you attract into your life, and there are only two options:

1. Wealth
2. Poverty

The middle class is shrinking, which leaves two classes:

1. The upper class
2. The lower class

Those who have are given more.
Those with less get what they have taken away.

Affirmations

Wealth is my divine right.

I was born to be wealthy.

Wealth continually attracts itself to me.

I can afford whatever I desire.

There are no limits to the amount of wealth I can create.

I am a wealth magnet.

New ideas that create wealth come to mind frequently.

I am a creator of wealth.

I only experience abundance.

. . .

Chapter 2

Focus On Abundance

Whatever you focus on you will attract.

If you focus your thoughts on lack, that will be your life experience.

If you focus your thoughts on abundance, that will be your life experience.

Are your thoughts rooted in lack or abundance?

Affirmations

I always focus my thoughts on abundance.

I am unfamiliar with lack because I repel it.

I experience more than enough on all fronts.

I was born with royalty in my blood.

It is my birthright to experience abundance.

I hold the financial reigns.

Financial relevance and power encapsulate me.

My endeavors flourish in every capacity.

I maintain an abundant mentality.

Abundance is mine for the taking.

...

Chapter 3

Eradicate Impoverished Thoughts

Broke people all have something in common: ***their thinking.***

*Frequent phrases **broke** people say:*

- *I'm broke.*

- *I can't afford that.*

- *How much is that?*

- *I never have enough.*

- *I'm barely getting by.*

- *That's expensive/pricey.*

- *That's out of my league.*

- *I wish I could afford that.*

Affirmations

1. I have everything I need to flourish.

2. Everything I desire is attracting itself to me.

3. I was born wealthy.

4. I am financially dominant.

5. I never explore impoverished thoughts.

6. My life is a treasure chest of success.

7. I cannot be anything but wealthy.

8. Wealth and I are best friends.

9. There is nothing out of reach for me.

10. Riches surround me.

. . .

Chapter 4

Happiness

The happiest people on earth are wealthy. Wealth does not only encapsulate riches, but wealthy relationships, health, and purpose.

When you are walking in your purpose, and living a life congruent with who you are, you will experience more happiness in your life, which will only attract more wealth.

Affirmations

1. I am flourishing in my relationships.

2. Inspiring, enriching, and wealthy people surround me.

3. I am flourishing in my health.

4. My body and mind are perfect.

5. I am flourishing in my life purpose and goals.

6. My purpose is continually unfolding before me because I refuse to let it die.

7. Gratitude is my anchor; it keeps me balanced.

8. I do not sacrifice my happiness for things and people who misalign with my values.

9. Life treats me too well to be unhappy.

. . .

Chapter 5

Leverage Your Gifts

Our gifts tell us which direction of life we should go in. Those who don't utilize their gifts are throwing away a multitude of wealth.

How can you start leveraging your talents and gifts?

Affirmations

1. The gifts I'm born with are indicators of my purpose.

2. I maximize the utilization of my gifts.

3. All my gifts are wealth creators.

4. There is an abundance of opportunities for me.

5. There is no limit to how I can utilize my gifts.

6. I am infinitely gifted and talented.

7. There is no other human being that can do exactly what I can do.

8. There are no limits to my potential.

9. None of my gifts go to waste.

Chapter 6

Focus On Creating -- Not Competing

There is more than enough for everyone. People who believe there is a limited supply of wealth are lying to themselves and spreading this gigantic lie to others.

If and when you believe there is more than enough, that shall be your life experience.

Never compete.
Always create.

Affirmations

1. I am a creator.

2. There is plenty for me and everyone.

3. What I wish for myself, I wish for others.

4. I do not measure myself against others.

5. I build wealth for myself and inspire others to do the same.

6. There is no shortage of wealth for me and everyone else.

7. There is an abundant and unlimited supply of abundance for the world.

8. I always experience more than enough.

9. Nothing substantial comes from competing.

. . .

Chapter 7

Let Go Of Fear

Fear is the number one stopper to wealth. If you don't believe you can experience riches, wealth, and financial surplus, you never will.

Most people don't dare to dream because they don't know how they will make the dream happen.

Don't focus on "how" to obtain wealth. Instead, focus on feeling wealthy, thinking wealthy, and exploring your talents and gifts.

Continually seek knowledge and write down ideas. You never know which idea or interaction will lead you directly to your dream.

Affirmations

1. *Fear has no hold on my mind, life, or actions.*

2. *I am determined to succeed in my endeavors.*

3. *Fear has no power in my life.*

4. *There is no room for poverty in my life.*

5. *I **can** experience wealth.*

5. *I embody a wealth mentality.*

6. *Abundance overflows my life.*

7. *I am economically immune to negative financial circumstances and outcomes.*

8. *There is such a thing as a life without fear, and I am living it today and always.*

. . .

Chapter 8

Generosity Is At The Core Of Wealth

The most giving people are the wealthiest people.

Those who don't give (due to whatever excuse they tell themselves) will never experience genuine wealth.

To be wealthy means to give to others abundantly and without fear.

Practice giving wherever you financially are (without hurting yourself) and notice the good that starts taking place in your life.

Generosity sits at the core of wealth creation.

When you give, the universe gives back to you most abundantly.

Affirmations

1. I am a lavish giver.

2. Giving opportunities find me wherever I go.

3. It feels better to give than to receive.

4. My heart, mind, and soul are generous.

5. I do not believe in holding on to everything I am given.

6. The universe is generous to me in every way.

7. I always have more than enough wealth to share with others.

8. When I give, the universe plants seeds that will return to me more than I gave.

9. I can never give too much.

. . .

Chapter 9

Action

There are ideas sitting in your brain that you have never executed or invested much time and energy into.

Explore the ideas that come to mind and write down each and every idea.

You never know which idea will be your $100,000 idea, $1,000,000 idea, $10,000,000 idea, $100,000,000 idea, or $1,000,000,000 idea.

Give everything a fighting chance. Some ideas won't work. Some ideas will produce traction. Some ideas will take off and fly.

Explore every idea.

Affirmations

1. I am productive with my time, effort, and energy.

2. I do not engage in lazy habits and behaviors that don't yield fruitful results.

3. Each day I give 100% effort to my dreams.

4. I never go to bed without investing time into my dreams.

5. I commit to making a little progress on my goals daily.

6. I am moving in the direction of wealth daily.

7. My ideas are creating more present and future wealth for me.

8. I am succeeding in every form.

. . .

Chapter 10

Wealth Is My Birthright

Whether you were born into poverty or economic distress, it is your birthright to experience and live a wealthy life.

Dream big and lead with big actions. Whatever you're seeking is seeking you.

If you're seeking wealth, know that wealth is also seeking you.

How will you attain it? It all starts with how you think and feel regarding wealth.

Everyone has the power and can create the opportunity to inject wealth into their lives.

What will you do?

Affirmations

1. I am a wealth creator.

2. Wealth is my natural birthright.

3. I choose to live wealthy.

4. I was born to be rich.

5. Wealth and riches are mine.

6. There is no better time than now to experience wealth.

7. Abundance is my birthright and experience.

8. I am comfortable with wealth, abundance, and a higher lifestyle.

9. Nothing can detract me from experiencing wealth.

. . .

The End

. . .

Thank You Note

Thank you for taking the time to read this book, and I appreciate the opportunity you have given me to invest in your life.

1% improvements every day will transform you into an elevated human being.

Continue investing in your life through reading and self-education.

About Destiny S. Harris

Destiny S. Harris' goal is to positively inspire, cultivate, elevate, and educate the minds of individuals across the globe through her writing.

With over 600+ books published to date, creating (whether books, courses, articles, poetry, or music) has always been Destiny's thing, not to mention health & fitness and all things entrepreneurial. Destiny published her first book, "Beauty Secrets for Girls," at age 11 and her second book, "Don't Wait Until It's Too Late," at age 12.

Destiny obtained three degrees from the University of Georgia in Psychology, Political Science, & Cultural Studies. She also started her own music teaching business at the age of 14, which she led for over ten years. In addition, she has been teaching academic, career, and personal development topics to thousands of students and readers since 2004.

Outside of writing, Destiny loves and enjoys a few other things: reading, bodybuilding, traveling, dogs, food, classic movies, anime, mountain and ocean views, plants, and nature.

Check out her work, leave a review, share your thoughts with your friends and family, and be a part of a movement: helping people learn and grow through means of self-education (books).

<u>Complete the Steps To Get Free eBooks:</u>

Step 1: Go to amazon.com/author/destinyharris

Step 2: Filter books by "Price: Low to High"

Step 3: Download available free books

Connect W/ Destiny S. Harris

Please reach out and stay in touch. Destiny S. Harris enjoys chatting with readers. Start a conversation today @ **linktr.ee/destinysharris**

Leave A Review

My goal is to positively impact as many lives across the globe as possible through my writing, and I need your help doing this.

One way you can help me is to leave a book review, which will continue to help spread the word about my books.

When you have a moment, please take the time to review this book.

Thank you in advance!

Share This Read

If you found this book valuable, please take the time to invest in someone else's life, share what you learned from this book, or loan your copy.

It's honorable to give.

It feels remarkable to give, and we mustn't keep all the good stuff to ourselves.

2nd Free Gift!

<u>Access My Free Courses & Books @</u>

linktr.ee/destinysharris